Advance Reviews

"Take the familiar and make it strange." (Thus spake short-story story writer Lydia Davis.) This is what poet Matt Hohner has done. Hohner hits the imaginative, intuitive nail on the head again and again in his collection *Thresholds*. Imagination leaps over time and space: for example, a poem's two footnotes cite rock supergroup U2 and the second century Chinese poet Lu Chi. Here is poetry for readers who admire intellect that works at gut level. For readers who love poetry. And readers who don't."

> — Clarinda Harriss, author of *The White Rail*, a short story collection, 6 poetry collections, and *The Innumerable Moons*, a collection of poetry and short fiction (forthcoming)

"In a distinct luminous voice, Matt Hohner's poems are a clairaudient cartography of the silent currents orbiting our lives. These poems map the tragic and profound events and memories that come not just to define us but to propel us toward hope. Charting the stars, the sea floors, the streets of Baltimore, 'the history raging around us,' *Thresholds* will carve its atlas on your heart."

> — Edgar Silex, poet, author of *Through All the Displacements* and *Acts of Love* (Northwestern University Press), and *Even the Dead Have Memories* (New Sins Press)

"The world, and Baltimore in particular, has been waiting for *Thresholds* for years, and *Thresholds* has been waiting for us... as friends, relatives, mentors, spouses, teachers, students, neighbors, victims, addicts, killers...as readers.

Matt Hohner's stunning collection is an immeasurable account of history, landscape, and humanity that is only visible through verse, where wars are simultaneously waged—internally and externally, where loss and love meet in the small ripple of a hidden river, where poetry is as painful as birth.

Thresholds brings us a blueprint made of "simple wooden boats and carts" and "acrid cloudsmoke scraping across an impossible sky," a place for remembrance, for validation, for mourning, longing, and fear. Here, we are given the chance to cross lines and limits, returning and moving forward, instinctually and unapologetically, toward home."

> — Katherine Cottle, author of three books with
> Apprentice House Press, *I Remain Yours*, *Halfway*,
> and *My Father's Speech*

"In *Thresholds*, Matt Hohner's muscular, clear-eyed poems draw a densely textured map: one reads, slipping into the poems' loci, their creeks and gorges, streets and dark skies. These are poems of deep fidelity: to memory and to place; to past hurts and the scars they've left; and to love. Hohner is unafraid of brutal truths: in one poem, the speaker says, of a mother, that he grows "no closer to her now/ than I would to a marble headstone, or a lie." But the poems do not shrink from the great beauties either, and this is their power. In 'Saratoga Passage,' the speaker says, 'I have known this pulling-to and letting go / I have known the searing white heat of entry into this world alone, / the profound momentary ripples, the lonely stillness that follows.' The stir, and the stillness, are the gifts these poems give us."

— Lisa Bickmore, author of *Ephemerist* (Red Mountain Press) and *flicker* (Elixir Press)

"Matt Hohner's *Thresholds* is an extraordinary collection of poems steeped in an awareness of history and culture and the natural world. With unflinching attention to detail, in a voice both angry and tinged with sadness, the poet decries the horrifying behavior of human beings in the contemporary world. In other poems, he explores the depths of friendship and family, personal loss and longing, and the healing that can best be found in love and nature. *Thresholds* reminds the reader that only by contemplating darkness can we truly appreciate the light."

— Bill Jones, poet, author of *Swimming at Night* (winner of the Artscape 1992 literary award) and *At Sunset, Looking East* (Apprentice House Press)

Thresholds

AND OTHER POEMS

Thresholds

AND OTHER POEMS

Matt Hohner

Apprentice
House Press
Loyola University Maryland

First Edition

Paperback ISBN: 978-1-62720-181-0
E-book ISBN: 978-1-62720-182-7

Printed in the United States of America

Design by Rebecca Dellinger
Marketing by Natalie McDonald
Development by Angela Longhi
Cover photo by Matt Hohner
Back cover author photo by Shannon Kline

Published by Apprentice House

Apprentice
House Press
Loyola University Maryland

Apprentice House
Loyola University Maryland
4501 N. Charles Street
Baltimore, MD 21210
410.617.5265 • 410.617.2198 (fax)
www.apprenticehouse.com
info@apprenticehouse.com

Acknowledgments

The author wishes to recognize and thank the original publishers of the following poems:

"Dream, July 5, 2006," *The Potomac*

"Gulf War Veteran," *Poets Against War* and *The Potomac*

"Under the Leonids," *End of 83*

"Terror in the Dust," *September Eleven: Maryland Voices*

"Oysters," *Enizagam* and winner of 2014 Maryland Writers Association Literary Contest

"Toward Pittsburgh," "Tornado Warning," "Noel Aubade," and "Gut," *Meat for Tea*

"Beaver Dam, 1987," Honorable Mention, 2016 Allen Ginsberg Poetry Award Sponsored by the Poetry Center at Passaic County Community College, *Paterson Literary Review*

"Columbia," *District Lit*

"Dundee Creek," *Potomac Review*

"Dundalk," *Clapboard House*

"The Maximum Effective Range," *Lily* and finalist in *The Lascaux Review* 2014 Prize in Poetry

"Psalm 40" and "Cord" *Mom Egg Review*

"Confirmation," *Truck*

"Kevin," *The Five-Two*

"Please Refrain from Celebratory Gunfire" and "In Memoriam Annum," *Free State Review*

"Ground Rules," finalist, Earl Weaver Prize, *Cobalt*

"Pulse," *the light ekphrastic*

"May Day," finalist for the *Sow's Ear Poetry Review* 2014 Poetry Prize

"Curfew," first place, *Oberon* Poetry Prize, *Oberon Poetry Magazine 2016*; short-listed, Fish Poetry Prize 2016

"Saratoga Passage, August 2014," *The Moth*, short-listed for the Ballymaloe International Poetry Prize and reprinted in *The Irish Times*; Winner of the 2015 *Lascaux* Prize in Poetry

"The Last Hours of Summer," Third Prize, 2014 Maryland Writers Association Literary Contest

"Phantom," *Oberon Poetry Magazine*

"When Living Well Isn't Good Enough, Invite Your Enemies to Dinner," *The Poeming Pigeon*

"Saudade: 1983," Honorable Mention, *New Millennium Writings* 40th *NMW* Awards

"GPS," *The Whale Road Review*

"To a Poet of the Three Gorges" and "Famine Memorial, Dublin," *Arlington Literary Journal*

"The Color of the Fluid in My Father's Catheter Reminds Me of Snowball Flavors," *Reed Magazine*

"Beauty," "Winter Storm Warning," and "What to Do When Someone Shoots Up a Gay Nightclub in Florida in the Name of God While You Are Living at an Artist Colony," *The Potomac*

"How to Unpack a Bomb Vest," *Rattle, Poets Respond*

"The Investment Building," finalist, 2017 Muriel Craft Bailey Award, *Comstock Review*

"Reverse Bachata," *Califragile*

Thresholds has garnered the following recognition:

Crab Orchard Series in Poetry First Book Award: semi-finalist

Backwaters Press Prize for Full-length Book Manuscript: finalist

Brick Road Poetry Press Book Contest: runner-up

Broadkill River Press Dogfish Head Poetry Prize: honorable mention

Additional Thanks

I owe numerous people a thousand bows for their help, encourage-
ment, and assistance in the making and shaping of these poems
and this book. I thank my father, sister, and my wife for being my
most bedrock supporters, both in life and in my pursuits. I thank
the luminous poets Bill Jones, Kathy Cottle, Clarinda Harriss,
Edgar Silex, and Lisa Bickmore for being early readers of this
manuscript, and for their comments and suggestions. Every pub-
lishing team who previously published many these works individ-
ually, some in earlier form, deserves immense gratitude for seeing
their worth and in sharing them with others. Thank you also to the
crew at Apprentice House Books for your care and labor in making
this book possible. Finally, I recognize and bow deeply to Naropa
University, and to my esteemed instructors there, including Anne
Waldman, Steven Taylor, Andrew Schelling, and, in memoriam,
Anselm Hollo, Joanne Kyger, Jack Collom, and Allen Ginsberg.

Some of the work in this book was written and edited during a res-
idency at the Virginia Center for the Creative Arts, made possible
by a grant from Mid Atlantic Arts Foundation.

For my wife
and for my father

Contents

...that my poems may approach the true measure of things and stand against the unbalance and ignorance of our times.

–Gary Snyder

Dream, July 5, 2006

Coyote has crept into the house
up from the ravine where he
has followed deer from the county
into the city along Herring Run.
I go to rescue the cat
in the living room, fend off
the intruder by kicking at it,
kicking my wife in her calf
as I thrash about asleep,
waking myself up with a laugh
as Jen punches me in the shoulder,
rolls over, and falls back to sleep.
At night, these predators
creep into our life like doubt,
wild, uninvited, but something
we live with, fence out, fend off
when it gets too close, and listen
to at dusk as it calls from far off,
lonely, seeking insecurity, its mate.
We shudder at its untamability,
its reminder to huddle close
against the darkness
just beyond our embrace.

Kevin

Has danced into class every day this year.
Some days, he's James Brown throwing off his cape;
others, he's pop-locking old-school style,
moon-walking, doing the Harlem shake, or leanin' wit it.

His eyes always smile, especially when goofing
to cope with the challenge of reading. Today,
something's wrong. I pull him into the hall and ask,
why the angry look, the sulking.

Two cousins shot on their stoop last night,
one dead, he and his brother having just
gotten up to leave, having just turned the corner
to walk the two blocks home.

This world of darkness, punctuated
by muzzle flashes and numbness,
has followed him on two different buses,
across district lines, into the good school
where his mother lied to get him away from it.

He had turned the corner,
but the world he left behind now sits
at the third desk back on the right,
its shadow eclipsing his eyes.

To A Poet of the Three Gorges

It is evening: cold wind, late November,
east side of Baltimore's harbor. In the display
window of an upscale home furnishings
boutique, an old wooden ox cart wheel,
circa 19th century China, mounted
on an iron stand: prized salvage
from the flooded towns and valleys where
the Yangtze carved deep into millennia,
cascading through culture and time.

I think of Du Fu, turning his ear
to the gibbons' howls reverberating
deep in the three gorges, his skiff
moored along the shore, verses coming
like lanterns at night, borne by the dark currents,
lifeblood of heritage, surging past his bow.

Downstream, a new power flows from the river,
its megawatt hum echoing off concrete ramparts.
The old voices, now whispers, drown in waters
rising to light cities of millions where, once,
men in simple wooden boats and carts
delivered the news one verse at a time.

Gulf War Veteran

When he returned
from the desert,
a former high school
classmate brought home
an extra pair of ears,
each taken from
confirmed kills.

He talked of stars'
brilliance through
night vision lenses,
of breathing acrid smoke
from the well fires
and coughing up
globs of blood and oil,
of scorpions seeking
drops of moisture
in soldiers' mouths
and stinging their tongues
as they slept.

Part of me died
that evening
when I saw him.

He never returned
from that war.

Under the Leonids

Two a.m., twenty-five degrees. Shivering on a
roadside between open fields on top of a hill,
I gaze east and up at November's mute fires,
magnesium streaks quick-etched across the night,
their glowing trails hanging like tiny hosannas of light
before dissolving back to heaven. Farther from earth,
satellites zip from horizon to horizon in silent orbit.
On the cold wind, a soft whiff of nitrates and damp soil
swirls with wood fire smoke from nearby farm houses.
The distant low roar of a passenger jet rises and falls.
Somewhere, a dog barks at deer shuffling through
the corn stubble. Minute under the vast and endless
river of stars, I watch with gratitude as sparks shoot
from the Lion's mane, heavenly travelers hurtling
through the darkness of time to crash hot to earth,
brief glories scratching the hours like static, fading
swift as dreams the moment we wake. Their ions,
like knowledge, linger to tease, then are gone.

Toward Pittsburgh

Night falls between mountain ridges,
open car windows and headlights on,
lullaby of tiresong beside cow farms,
faded Mail Pouch Tobacco billboard
painted on the side of an old barn.
Fragrant alfalfa breath of summer
darkness settles like gossamer hands
enfolding a postage-stamp grass meadow,
edge of the woods by the interstate
south of Breezewood and the Turnpike;
U2's "Promenade" pulses low on the car stereo,
and you, behind the wheel, steady as years.
Light by quiet light, Edward Hopper's America
nestles into its small, white, box houses,
blue glow of computer and TV screens
spilling out through upstairs bedroom curtains.
Slide show, seaside town. Coca-cola, football radio,
radio, radio, radio, radio, radio ...
Thin fog hugs the farm fields' edges;
fireflies glitter the treetops:
hold this moment, a little longer.

Terror in the Dust

September, streets capsizing,
spilling over, down the drain.
Shards of glass, splinters like rain
   –U2, "Please"

It is more than any one of us can bear.

On a cloudless, warm day, burning people
drop from windows spewing smoke,
each tiny face reconciled with death,
falling one hundred stories through the air.
An upside-down business man, arms at his sides
and legs straight, tie flapping in the wind;
a man and woman holding hands. Americans.
Americans–pelting the concrete like hail.
On the ground, a fireman sees his colleague
crushed by a falling body. Airline passengers,
human shrapnel in the hands of madmen,
land blocks away still strapped to their seats.
Then time itself melts before our eyes
in a pyroclastic, nightmare roar, leaving
behind a hole in the sky.

It is more than any one of us can bear.

Ashen clouds of pulverized concrete
billow through the canyons of Manhattan,
sprinkling the powdered lives of thousands
on the helmets of saints who choke in the morning
twilight on asbestos plumes and vaporized marble,
on the odor of death and melted steel.

Crushed cars are buried to their roofs in debris.
A million reams of paper drift on subway steps
as the wind scatters DNA all the way to Brooklyn.
A tooth, an arm, a hair; a wedding finger glinting in the dust.
Fragments of life in the unimaginable tonnage of loss.

To a poet, there is terror in the dust.[1]

Blinking red lights in kitchens across the globe:
cell phones carried their voices–
desperate goodbyes left behind on answering machines.

We wear their names like heart attack scars,
endure the terrible day like victims of rape.

It is more than any one of us can bear.

Words move into the shadows and vanish;
memory returns in an echo of silence.

There are times when the spirit freezes,
feels dead as bleached wood
and dry as a riverbed in drought.

For a way out, we search the depths of our souls
for a spirit; beg for a vital sign of life.[2]

We are given only this:

> Outside in the lush, late summer afternoon,
> the first yellow leaves of autumn
> flutter gently to the ground.

Baltimore
September 11, 2001

Dundee Creek

Motionless over a meadow of bay grass,
the kayak's hull is tickled by mossy
leaves waving in tidal currents. Fish
jumps, circles fan out. Poplar trunks,
cattails; two power plant smokestacks
striped red and white tower over the marsh.

Signs along the Proving Ground shore warn
trespassers against unexploded ordnance,
as all the wars waged against others
are first waged against ourselves.

Blue heron stalks the grenade shallows;
men cast lines into dangerous depths.
Minnows scatter when paddle blades
slice the brackish calm.

Columbia[3]

High atmosphere space bounce
in transit beneath dawn moon's pallid glow,
galactic dazzle and dream talk breaking up
as ambient creatures return on earthbound comet.

Human particles once alive with love
and skill and care skip across ozone—
inside becomes outside nanoseconds at a time.

Entrails of carbon and junk flare and flash
through the heat barrage, the hearts of nations
boom and crash into gravity's deathly grip
at twelve times the speed of sound.

Data smeared across radar and heaven,
a brushstroke of dust on the edge of moment
glares, gleams, and streaks toward home.

Dundalk

Slow burn of rust across the eyelids of old men
decades out of the plant, rooted on torn leather stools
in the darklight at Minnick's, underneath the shadows
of the Seagram's plant's hulking brickwall desolation
and splintered floors echoing junkies and johns having sex.

A left shoe soaking in the rain out back of Penn Central,
where the creosote odor of rotting ties wraps around
a white wooden cross, *Too Soon* inscribed across its chest,
poking stark like bones out of the needles and potato chip bags
in the trackside weeds. A three-legged mongrel tightens
at the end of its chain in a dirt yard, barks all night
at trains rumbling slowly east past tenements and tents,
pounding through the neighbors' alcohol sleep.

A wet easterly breath off the water, carrying the sewage
stench of the treatment plant, mudflats of dumped tires
at low tide, the dry hack of toxic dust over Bear Creek
from the tailings of Sparrows Point's last convulsive blasts
of furnace and steel, over mercury sludge hiding enough crabs
for someone to pull out on chicken necks, steam for dinner,
ignore the metallic taste, swig it down with beer.

The children raise themselves in anger and show up
for school doped on mom's pills, unshowered and late,
cussing like absentee longshoremen fathers they never met,
hope flickering there behind dark inlets of eyes seeking love,
heartbeats begging routine, arms flailing for a hug
and punching at walls they cannot see. Tough.
Scratch it. Underneath the skin, Job's blood courses
through lava veins where it is still warm, the soul breathing,
singing in joy at dawn for the promise of another day,
clamoring through all the damage to a heart still beating
to the rhythm of lunar ebbs, shift whistles, stirring to the sound
of acrid cloudsmoke scraping across an impossible sky.

The Maximum Effective Range

for the victims at Virginia Tech, April 16, 2007

The diameter of the bullet is .22 inches
and the distance of its maximum effective range
is thirty yards, but further when fired by anger
fueled with paranoia, curving with the earth,
falling in a graceful, parabolic arc, unlike these
thirty-two dead, one suicide, twenty-six wounded.
The muzzle flash of a Walther P22 discharging
one hundred rounds is orange; the results maroon,
spilling out into a hallway from under a dorm room door.
In an expanding color wheel of panic and space:
thirty hungry ambulances, three hundred terrified parents,
a shocked nation of three hundred million.
But the old man who holds the door closed against the fury,
inches and moments from death, sixty-two years removed
from the six million dead of Auschwitz, of Buchenwald,
reduces the maximum effective range in a classroom considerably,
while the echoes of the shots and the moans of the dying
carried by the howling winds of that day
reach distant shores far across an ocean named for peace,
and the maximum effective range of the sounds
somehow amplified and heard by heaven,
washes over the ears of an unrelenting God.

Gut

Jen and I turn our kayaks off the Wicomico River
and up a narrow corridor of seven-foot marsh grasses
just wide enough for our paddles, past nests of marsh wrens,
pouches hung from bent reeds, past snags of fallen branches,
eagles and osprey streeling away from treetop roosts
as we approach. Through methane stink of tidal mud berms,
rotten fish, runoff from chicken farms a half-mile inland,
we parallel an uninhabited island of pines and scrub,
twisting off and doubling back again, toward the pond
the local man said was there, far back. A mile into the gut,
the alley of reeds opens to sky, warm sun, cooling breeze.
In two days, we will be married three years,
together thirteen, known each other almost twenty.
We fan out to either side of the pond, look across
to each other, smiling, having made it this far.

During the Mexican Revolution, Slain Catholic Rebels Were Strung from Telegraph Poles[4]

The ground was so close,
he could jump from that height
and not hurt his feet upon landing,
yet the cool, inviting earth
was miles away
and his breath drew shorter
as the makeshift noose
tightened with his weight.

Digits numb, bound limbs
tingling with sleep,
the Resistance now reduced
to futile flaps and twitches
and gurgles from the gunshot wound
in his chest,
he glared in desperation
at the next man down
swaying gently
in the hot September wind,
the struggle already gone
from his body.

There, high above the muffled land,
he decided that to die alone
had dignity
and the ruffle of his pants
became an organ,
the creak of the rope
a quiet sermon,
his swollen tongue
his last communion.

Psalm 40

for my birth mother on my fortieth birthday

I am listening online to a song no human has heard
before: a red giant's firelight rearranged into sound
waves, its pulses crossing the cold light years to earth.
It is the throbbing sound of blood pumping through veins,
the sound inside a womb of a mother I have never known.

Was it the same for you forty years back, my birth
a sound you'd never heard? A hard sound sharper
than scalpels, cutting a hole in you the size of God,
pulling you apart at the atoms, the silence
afterward only forgiveness could fill?

It is said that red stars are largest just before
collapsing in on themselves, a strange sort of birth
of the absence of light, where time bends and slows
to a stop, where nothing escapes, not even love.

I am listening to an old song
last heard through placenta and bone
from a warm universe long since forgotten
except by you—the pain of that day, the sound
of a black hole forming in your heart
where a son used to be.

Hail Mary

By now the trees have sloughed off
most of summer. Streetlights in the old
neighborhood glow at 4:00 p.m. It is
early November. Thirty-five autumns ago,
we lined up at scrimmage on that perfect
gridiron flat field next to Babcock church
in a raw, driving rain. Two oaks thick as
cannons goal-posted one end zone; two
silver maples, the other. Big Sean's blitz
was lightning fast, but your rubber legs
carried you free of the sack. You were
Jim Plunkett. You were Johnny Unitas.
In three weeks you will be dead five years.
Rather than think of you taking flight
from the edge of Eldorado Canyon, I
remember that beaten-smooth pigskin,
mid-sky, a Hail Mary issued into the wind
as Sean flattened you into the soft muck,
my stiff, numb hands raised in supplication
into the storm of you, diving into your
twilight to make one last miracle catch.

Ground Rules

In the small field outside Steve's house on the grounds
of the church where his dad preached, first base was a bare patch
of dirt by the rusty fence; second base, a rotten railroad tie across
the driveway that on hot days reeked of creosote; third, a metal
trash can lid dropped in the grass. A home run made it in the air
into Steve's yard, or pounded off the aluminum siding of the
chapel where Alcoholics Anonymous met, behind which Steve
would smoke pot and drop acid all through high school. Over the
chapel roof, grand slam. Ring the bell in the open belfry, win the
game—instant walk-off, regardless of inning. Any ball we couldn't
snag before the runner touched second, ground-rule double. Fouls
went past the trees in left; over the alley fence in right. Put-outs
at home were thrown over home plate before the runner scored.
Phil spray painted the rough average of our stances as a strike zone
on plywood set against the fence behind the batter when Brian,
in his hockey pads and mask, wasn't around to catch. How many
times did Steve's dad scold us for diving after screaming line drives
into his century-old boxwoods? How many hard slides into home
in shorts to earn a win and road rash that lingered for days?
The dents on that chapel have outlived Steve and his father. Our
diamond now grows a community garden. The four of us played
those humid dusks until well after the lightning bugs began to
dance for mates in the infield that last fleeting summer, before we
retired our bats and gloves, the four bases shifted from our dirt field
to girls' mysterious bodies, and the ground rules for everything
became lessons we'd spend our lives trying to unlearn.

Pulse

A cold north wind knifes south, Chihuahuan dust
chafing his eyes too desiccated to close. The distant trill
of a flute dances into his ears as his empty veins collapse,
hollow heart slows, ants begin to soldier into his wounds.
If only he could climb out of the arroyo, collect his blood
clotting in the soil, walk home. He notices how autumn
has brought sparrows to the phone lines above him. He
can hear the hum of conversations pulsing in the black
wires above his head as the whisper catches in his throat
just below the cut, *escalera, por favor*. The birds are silent.
He thinks of his mother's table, of poblanos and agave,
his last shot of tequila the night they came for him. He
thinks of Sunday morning mass, of the crucifix above
the altar, of padre's gentle, creased palms as they placed
the Eucharist on his tongue in the old adobe chapel
with the broken wood doors. A glassless window glows
above the birds where the sun should be as sky and earth
become a symphony of colors. The light in the window
sears him with love. One by one, the sparrows let go
of the words throbbing between their toes and become
song, lifting the afternoon into evening.

May Day

I walk out into a humid morning, my hand
curled around the rim of the skateboard. I hear
my mother's voice on Miss Ellen's porch. She's
chatting, hand pinching a cigarette thrown back
in the air, la-dee-da. She's been there for an hour or so.
I look over as I lock the door that is no longer hers
and wonder why she hasn't knocked at our house first.
"Hi, Mom," I say, across houses and years. She turns
and begins to answer, "Hi Hon–" as I drop four steps
off the top of the porch and land bang on the sidewalk,
click-clack seven squares to the curb, pop an ollie
onto the asphalt where she pulled away in her
rust-orange Datsun on May Day three years back.
I carve right, hard, wheels sliding, and haul ass
down the street, shoving the earth away with each push,
spinning the planet faster in reverse with each kick, raging
time backwards like Superman, to right before the sky
over me turned tornado green, and I understood at ten,
the end of love, the wreck of family, the limits of God.
Wheels growling beneath me, I roll away from her
into that summer's nuclear-winter fallout drift,
that long, slow, steady Geiger-counter tick of hurt.

God of Storms

Time where the tides rage
And roll like dream monsters
toward dead harbors, sounding far stations
Closed forever

—Thomas McGrath, *Letter to an Imaginary Friend*

Waves recede into the cold, into the deep. The world is quiet and damp
with the sound of the dying: breath among steel beams, splintered trees,
puddles of sludge. In the kitchen of his tilted and flood-wrecked house,
an old man finds a fish from miles out in the north Pacific. Nightmare
of Dali: the rudder of a fishing boat has crushed the skull of a horse;
both horse and vessel thrust skewered into the sky on the jutting ribs
of a car park stripped of its concrete flesh and bleeding gasoline and rust.

Echoes thunder along the coast: the God of Storms coughs hot atoms
into the air. Where Basho trod his long walk, dipping his gourd in the
river of stars, now the slow creep of isotopes shrouding what lingers
in a half-life measured by millennia. Twittering bitter click of the Geiger
counter ticks Saint Vitus' mad dance on a kaze[5] borne of hell. Bread lines
grow with silent specters, shocked monuments of gaman[6] whose genes
endured the deafening scorch roar of Hiroshima and Nagasaki.

Waterline scrawled across rooftops: ocean's angry signature. Stagnant
pools for eyes to weep the dead. In the twilight of dawn, crows and gulls
peck through the rot, getting fat. Concussed shadows move, bruised,
into razor-sharp sunlight, cutting thin forms amidst the rising odors.

The ground shakes again. The shadows stagger, punch-drunk. Grass fields
shimmy into toxic lakes, hillsides melt to gelatin, temples of wood and stone
become morgues. The God of Storms stirs in his sleep, dreaming of bones.

Fukushima Prefecture,
Tohoku, JapanMarch 11, 2011

Thresholds

For I am grateful, her love makes me humble.

–Sam Hamill, "Jubilate Sutra"

1.

I have learned that grace
arrives in moments and pulses,
clear true notes that cut through
the static and noise of everyday life.
I have found that to surrender myself
completely is an act of liberation,
that to ask of you is not to steal.

I have seen love transform
misery to comfort, anger to joy.

The year September eleventh
buried the anniversary of our first date
under piles of dust and bone and smoking steel,
I reached up through my grief and despair
and found your hand; I cried out and heard
the sound of your voice, the peace of love
answering through the din of streeling
rescue beacons and screaming men.
The act is done. The ache remains. We endure.
The anniversary of a beginning, not an end.

We carry each other over thresholds
of weakness and doubt, dress our wounds
with bandages of faith, wear our scars
with dignity and hope. This love is defiant.
This love is real. This love is possibility
in a world of negation. This love is a gift
we give to each other for the other's sake,
to fill each other through the gift of self.

This love is a promise kept, a meteor storm
born years ago and far away, falling to earth,
as certain as November's bright leonids,
through black cold toward each other,
our selves fusing as one doubled thing,
sacred mysteries in each other's arms.[7]

We fall into a love renewed every day.
We fall, and falling, are given wings.[8]

2.

Where the rooms were once empty
in the old brick house on the edge of urban woods,
the rooms silent, the walls lifeless and cold,
our conversations spill through open doors,
water bangs in the pipes, and a tide of boxes
swells and recedes as the old is put away
and gifts for a new life arrive.

Lately I've developed a taste for the quiet life:[9]
to light candles and draw you a warm bath;
to lie and talk together through the night;[10]
to fold spinach and portobellos into omelets
while you sleep in on Sundays; to sort laundry
while telling jokes; to know the specific creak
of the hallway floorboards as you move about
getting ready for work. To share this life
of infinite moments. To know I am not alone.

Storm clouds lumber east in midafternoon.
Across College Avenue the seventy-foot black locust
tosses green leaves into the humid gusts, its boughs
nodding and swaying as the sky thickens with rain:
recalling years ago, the storm we raced north into Utah
as darkness and lightning closed in around our car.

The edge of the Grand Canyon, your face soft
and golden and glistening with sweat, fingers
of sunlight reaching down through evening clouds,
hot air punctuated by the crorks of ravens
riding the dry thermals in concentric circles
up from the red and ochre cliffs. Fugitive
hours now ephemeral flashes, drifting
further away and into the past.

Expansive. Unconquerable. Undeniable.

Our first night in our new house, cool odor
of damp soil sifting through the window
after heavy rain, a lone fox barking hoarsely
in the wooded ravine as we drift off
to the swollen shush of Herring Run.

Endless cycle. Clarity of time.

3.

In the blink of your hazel eyes
I live a thousand lifetimes;
in your tears, I die a thousand deaths.
Your sighs are those of an archangel
gazing on a world gone mad.
I am elevated by the words you speak
and humbled by your daily kindnesses.
Your laughter heralds the birth of a million stars;
the cadence of your stride marks the beat of my heart.

Hyperbole. Exemplar. Simple truth.

I aspire to your gentleness, take solace
in your smooth and ageless patience.
I celebrate the privilege of your presence
minute by blessed minute. I become familiar
with a gratitude I have never known.

In the scintillation of your movement through space
you leave behind the essence and hope of all the saints
and wandering spirits in this most unholy time;
In your words and deeds you give me strength
in the wasteland of this savage and wretched planet.
In this *secret communication of untellable love*,[11]
I am soothed in my darkest hours of desolation.
When I call out your name, o holy and blessed wife,
I hear myself improved in the echo of your reply.

When Living Well Isn't Enough, Invite Your Enemies to Dinner

Revenge is best served in a cold, crisp salad:
a bed of jimsonweed and wolfsbane leaves,
sprinkled sparingly with belladonna berries for beauty and taste
and sliced death cap mushrooms layered liberally for oomph.
Chopped bloodroot for a peppery zing;
castor beans for a fresh, ricin crunch.
Garnish with digitalis—so delicate, so pretty!
Eat with lead utensils; tidy up with napkins
made from poison ivy pulp.
Dress it in a light, creamy rattlesnake venomette.
Wash it down with a cool glass of hemlock tea.
For desert, mistletoe ice cream!
After dinner, relax, kick back, and smoke
a whole bushel of raw, unfiltered tobacco.

Oysters

*At night—the soft shuck of everything on earth softly sliding away
into space.*

—Mary-Alice Daniel, "Hyperreality"

Every now and then you emerge from the soil,
exhumed out of the darkness by a backhoe
on a street in Baltimore. There you are. A body part,
serial-killed by history. An ear who last alive heard
the water-muffled splash of steam-driven paddle wheels.

A layer of flat calcium flakes under the asphalt
and macadam, under bricks and cobblestones.
Strata of progress. Archaeology of amnesia.

On a February rainy night in Annapolis you beckon
from ice in market stalls and raw bars barnacled in your
old-man skin, haired by algae, moist protein bodies inside,
dressed ugly, but the locals' lusty gazes shuck you with their eyes.

Bullets punched outboards and chests
over you. Men died for your flesh.

A beach on the Wicomico down from Salisbury where
the old packing plant once stood: kayakers tread your bones
to get to the tannin'd currents racing past. Women's hands
eighty-years dead last held you, dispatched your silent,
blind, bivalve lives inside with a poke-slip of their knives.

John Smith said he could walk across your shoals at low tide.
You have run aground many a foolish captain who lost track of you.

Once your legion filtered the whole bay in days; now
it takes you a year. There's mercury in the mud. There's lead.
How do you taste without that metallic after-singe?

Give me that cool glide at the back of my throat.
Give me your pornographic flavor.

I'll eat you until my blood runs silver.

Tornado Warning

8:00 p.m.

On the Weather Channel, a red crawler
warns of a funnel cloud on the ground,
a bow echo where winter and spring
waltz themselves into a deadly fury,
moving northeast through farmland
west of the city. I sip my rum drink
on the dark porch in the rain, wait
for your call, and pray for wind.

10:00 p.m.

Clouds race across the sky after the storm,
their bellies a peach city-lit under-glow.
Down in the ravine, swollen Herring Run
rushes deep and angry, the sound reaching
up the steep slopes in the darkness.
The air is warm and wet, open, like
the mouth of a lover, like a wound.

Midnight

The house is quiet with sleep.
My hand rests on your hip, my palm
cupping your bone, that perfect jab,
sharp peak jutting over smooth womb.
I close my eyes, listen to the distant rumble
of thunder, and dream of debris.

Vernal Nocturne

Frog song in the creek ditch:
spring peepers seek mates
in the dim, chill shade,

north side of Satyr Hill road,
up the steep incline to the ridge top,
low spine that sees to the bay.

Late light in the woods
lingers in new emerald sheen
after cold spring rain.

It is something like hope
that calls me into the gloaming,
makes my footfalls solid again

after a winter of little snow
and too much death.

Somewhere, groping webbed hands
and bodies breathing through skin
blindly reach one another
to begin again.

Beaver Dam, 1987

On a hot day in June when you are fifteen
or sixteen and male in mid-Atlantic humid
America, you do things with your friends
like decide it's a good idea to go swimming
at the quarry, so you get beer, park a half-mile
away, and sneak in the back way from the railroad
tracks in broad daylight, buzzing hard from the beer
and your own bold, youthful stupidity, striding
like kings out of the woods by the tracks
past the swimming pools to the old lake,
no one the wiser, and at forty-four you forget
what you talked about while you teetered
on and off the rails, chugging cans of Coors
and listening for trains, remembering only
that it felt right and good, and that the universe
had made that day for you, that the sun beating
on your skin was kind, lighting the world just so,
for you, granting you permission to do whatever
the fuck you wanted, that paying six bucks each
at the gate was an outrage, the cloudless sky
reflecting your dumbass conscience, as you
jostled to the T-bar swing, the rocking steel
buoys, the fifty-foot diving platform that plunged
you deep into the cool watery twilight where the sun
failed to reach, and you paused with two strong,
full lungs to remind yourself of something you'd lost
long, long ago, before kicking toward the surface
and the waning afternoon for air, for another jump
while there was still time, for one more leap
into the hazy, forgiving, ageless perfection
of the time of your giddy, clueless lives.

World Series

Memorial Stadium, 33rd Street, Baltimore

We sat in the top row, metal bleachers,
just left of home plate, Game 2, 1983.
Before the game, my father, his printer
friend, and I ate in a crowded, dimly lit
Chinese place in Waverly. Two Phillies
fans in maroon caps with white P's hunched
over their lo mein at the table next to ours,
glancing nervously over tight shoulders.
The food was exotic, salty, unfamiliar
to my twelve-year-old tongue. Of the
game I remember the deafening crowd,
Wild Bill Hagy drunk and shirtless in
Section 34, and an Orioles win. I don't
remember what we talked about, what
I wore, or who pitched, but I still carry
those moments long since hammered
to dust by wrecking balls and progress,
when my father and I lost our delirious
voices in the world's loudest outdoor
insane asylum as men in a timeless
game played out our dreams on a field
dissolved into memory, witnessed
from what is now air a hundred feet
above an otherwise insignificant street.

Cord

I am eight years old, running through the house
from the living room to the dining room, under
the taut phone cord and into the kitchen. My
mother is talking with a girlfriend from Sweet
Adelines. She's chain smoking, sitting in the slat
wooden swivel chair at the end of the faded grey
formica counter. The warm June afternoon light
spilling from the back yard into the hazy row
house beckons, but I stay inside to be near
her. She talks for hours on the phone, her lifeline,
drawing lit end after lit end into her lungs. The
coiled line stretches and tightens with her tone
as it follows her into another room when she
needs to whisper. I duck under that cord a half
dozen times for the attention she won't give me
before she sends me out into the yard with the dog.
How much longer would I hear her voice in that
kitchen, yank desperately on the line that keeps
us apart, that keeps her tethered to our home?
How much longer would the smoke of her
conversations linger in the air, a sure sign
of something burning in that house?

Phantom

At the bottom of Poplar Hill Road, the darkness still closes in
thick around your headlights like a slow thunderclap, like
silence after a muzzle flash. The trees who bore witness then
are taller. Three decades ago a secret crept out of the forest
to tell itself, then melted back into oblivion. You think of those
rainy spring nights in 1983. You think of desire and isolation.
You think of life returning in the woods, mating songs
of tree frogs and insects, timid hoof steps of deer far back
in the thickets. The roadside where they parked is still wild.
You think of the songs on their radios those nights. Some say
he knew the woods. Some say he raged at his own loneliness.
Cresting the hill where that peculiar old farmhouse turns its bruised
shoulder to the road, you think of gentle breaking sounds: footsteps on
wet leaves; ballads crackling inside steamed car windows at night.

Driving at Night to My Mother's House the Day After Christmas

Highway 29 south, middle of Virginia, cool
drizzle and fog, light traffic. Both of us quiet,
side-by-side. My wife's small hands hold the
wheel steady as truth, Radiohead swirling
from the speakers: *everything in its right place*....
Every few minutes, an inflatable snowman
or a plastic manger scene set back from the road,
glowing under a tree strung with lights, punctuating
the painful miles of darkness between Kwik Marts.
We are halfway to my mother's house, where
Parkinson's takes more of her year by year,
and she forgets and slurs, shakes and stumbles
closer to gone. I grow no closer to her now
than I would to a marble headstone, or a lie.
Damp asphalt vanishes beyond the round
arc of our high beams. Christmas lights
shimmer like a mirage on a distant slope,
promising nothing in an ocean of black.

Beauty

She stops what she is doing
at the entrance to the boutique
food market, bathed in gourmet
aromas from the stands inside,

reaches into her purse at her feet
to pull out a brush and comb her unruly
hair in the stifling subtropical air,
the sun now gleaming like a promise
through the rain clouds, parted
just so, for a moment,

makes herself presentable, her
short-sleeve shirt tucked neatly, evenly,
into her blue denim jeans that hug
narrow hips and concave stomach,

before unfolding the discreet cardboard
sign she'd tucked under her arm
that reads, *homeless god bless*
in bold, black letters
on crisp white background,

and turns to face the oncoming traffic
of her life and what it has become.

As I Think of You in Italy

The modem lights flutter like fireflies tapping out Morse code
in green pulses—information—information—*what do you know
at 1:30 in the morning, alone in your office in humid America,
the cat sleeping downstairs?* Peter Gabriel's New Blood
Orchestra's thrumming rendition of "In Your Eyes,"
the old and wizened voice strong as ever, flows
from the speakers, a monsoon of sound and love,
and I remember now, through those years, some twenty ago,
on a date at Sander's Corner, the restaurant below Loch Raven Dam.
Or was it twenty-four years ago—so young—high school, at the
movie about a kickboxer and the brainy beauty, her father the thief?
It was ten years ago also, in a marble holy place, your white dress,
words exchanged becoming covenant. Tonight there is an ocean
between us for the first time, salt-same as blood and tears,
and in your ears the language of your ancestors, dry wind,
history. In the bottom of the coffee mug you left on the desk,
the last sips you never take. I think of words unspoken.
I think of the sound of hearts beating, of drums. I think
of you in the world, and the cold bed I will collapse into
for a scant few hours of sleep, alone in the house we have fought
so hard to keep through earthquake and floods, anger and hurt,
hurricanes and isolation, blizzards and resentment, gunfire and loss.
In the dark I will reach for you across time and space, but my hand
will fall to empty sheets in the cool comfort of the air conditioner
window unit, ceiling fan turning a column of damp night
down upon my tired skin.

GPS

On the seat-back monitor in front of me, I
watch the icon of our passenger jet crossing
the North Atlantic on a red-eye from Philly
to Dublin. Names strange and familiar appear
in the blue zone between brown continents:
Gloria Ridge. Charlie Gibbs Fracture Zone.
Porcupine Plain. Great Meteor Tablemount.
Secret landscapes hidden deeper than lunar
knowledge. The map on the tiny flat screen
shows the rises and trenches, canyons crossed
by species no human has seen. Then, every
few minutes, oceanography gives way to the
names of vessels lost in war and storms. Mary
Rose, her guns sent swimming by the French.
Battle-scarred Colossus, run aground. Alabama,
pounded by the Kearsarge, in the front yard
of Europe. Treasure of the Douro, the glitter
of her diamonds folded into the velvet pockets
of the deep. Titanic's ice-borne tomb. Lusitania
and Carpathia, torpedoed in war. Thresher's
last dive to a uranium grave with all hands,
crushed like a tin can, her isotopes sifting like
radioactive pollen into the eyes of Poseidon.
The names mark the losses—dots on a map,
human lives vanished under miles of seawater.
I could run my fingers over the Atlantic's floor,
feel the jagged mountain ranges and hot volcanic
faults. I could caress the bones of civilizations
resting in silt finer than moon dust, exoskeletons
of tiny life drifting down like snow through
the lightless silence of ages. I could reach
into the pixels at forty-thousand feet, cradle
them to the surface, bring them home.

After Ibsen's *Hedda Gabler* at the Abbey Theater

Dublin, Ireland

The late air is cool, gentle salt whiff of the sea riffling
the Liffey's currents. Dublin: *black pool*. Etymology
for a thousand-year-old word now a half-submerged
pipe peering from stone and concrete. Hedda, too,
walled herself in, thrashed about, ended herself
before the iron-cold shackles of patriarchy and grace
closed forever around her delicate wrists. How we
solve our need for freedom; how we wall up what's
free to suit our needs. In Belfast this summer, they'll
ignite the firmament with bonfires, searing blindness,
the hot glow of vengeance scaling the high escarpments
built between the followers of Jesus to keep them apart.
My wife reaches across the sidewalk between us to take
my hand as we stroll to the river. A blade of moon cuts
the night east, her shadowed body visible in the rare,
clear sky; next to her, Venus punches through the darkness.
Gravity and love, cold shadows made darker by the light
that casts them—holding us together, setting us free.

Famine Memorial, Dublin

Smudges of Liffey's silt shuffle towards
the coffin ships, eye sockets plucked of sight.
There are no wailing keeners here to mourn
these shadows rising like wisps of peat smoke
from the cobbled walk. The dirges are long
gone from the rigored moors, sunken trenches
carved across the heart of Ireland where clans
interred their stories and thatched roofs hushed
into ruin. Under April's bright sun, the buds
of spring in the trees lining the riverbank,
waiflike parentheses mark the barren spaces
and unspoken sighs of cultural hurt: always
there, that void in the gut that faith once filled,
whence song took flight into the Atlantic wind.

Noel Aubade

Christmas morning. The cat is soft and curious, fed, and creeping
towards the butter on the counter as I cook eggs. Outside,
the backyard is a field of white surrendering to a gunmetal
sky that will bring flooding rain at any moment.

Footprints left two nights ago in the front yard
show where a gamboling fox romped after the storm,
hunting mice running between grass blades under the drifts.

My wife stirs upstairs. In the old oak across the street
at the edge of the Herring Run woods, the hot shock
of a cardinal punctuates the pewter sentence of a low branch.

The neighbor's house is dark and still. The eggs are done.
Rain starts to pitter-pat the windows. The cat licks my ankle,
her tongue the texture of wet sandpaper and warm love.
My wife's feet creak the wooden stairs, coming down.

Please Refrain from Celebratory Gunfire[12]

Tomorrow at midnight they will come out
onto their porches, into their yards.
They will point their guns toward
the stars and fire until they hear *click*
and go back inside to wash down
the gunpowder taste on their tongues
with brut and beer. Their rapid-fire
reports will linger sporadically
long after the fireworks from the harbor
crescendo with their sustained thunder.
On New Year's Day the news will tell us
of someone's skull splitting—*kachuk*—
as revelers miles away turned to find
a body collapsed lifeless on the ground.

Tomorrow night I will listen in the charged air
and wait for the stars to fall from holes
where they were shot out
of the night like the eyes of gods
we have all long since forgotten
to thank for the round earth, gravity,
the brains to measure the trajectory
of seasons, the sense to get out
of the way of our own history,
the foolishness to repeat it time
and time again as our intentions
come crashing back to earth in a heap
and wait for dawn's cold light to bathe us
with the promise of living another year.

Clairaudient

June 1989

Three hits of acid before 11:00 a.m., black caves
of blown-out pupils eclipsing emerald irises: *I'm lost*,
you said. *I can't find my house*. Sinking into the cobalt
armchair in my living room, glassine eyes watching a movie
miles away in a place I couldn't see: *I just need to get home*,
you sighed, melting into the patterned fabric of the cushions.
You don't remember where you live? I asked. *I remember my house*,
but I know this isn't my street, you answered, amused
by red brick row houses and black rooftops swirling together,
familiar streets and yards dissolving into rainbow Silly Putty
dreamscapes. Your face drained blank as I sat across from you
and watched, wondering how fucked up a man had to be to get lost
in his own neighborhood two blocks from home. The minutes oozed:
five…ten…. I watched you breathe, catatonic. Then, grip loosening
on the chair, arms bending at the elbows, hands raised in proclamation
—or surrender—your face lit up like a television set: *Phone's ringing!*
No, Steve, I began to answer, *It isn—* when the phone rang once,
bursting into the cool shade of the front room like a car alarm.
See, you said, nonchalantly. *I told you the phone was ringing*.
After a glass of Kool-Aid you said tasted like Smurfs, I walked
you as far as the boulevard. Bounding wildly across the four
lanes like a rubber scarecrow in a wind storm, you somehow
made it across, leaving me standing on the near shore of a
vast river widening between us, never to be crossed again.

Confirmation

for Klaude

Penance

What is the sound
of regret through the wind
at sixteen feet per second?

Absolution

Your feet, empty
as beams of light.
Your smile a dead
giveaway.

Resurrection

The stone moved aside.
An empty tomb.
She found your burial clothes
laid out neatly on your bed.

Age of Discretion

You must have wanted
as I stood with you
before Christ.
You must have known.

Lead us not.
Lead us not into.
Lead us.

Sanctum

In a car. On a lot. In the daylight. You paid the boy.
You hated yourself. Your prayers were flagellants.

Persecution

You were drunk in the car when they pulled you over.
They brought you before the judge. You were guilty. You fled.
They crucified you in the news. I denied your name to myself.
You were drunk in the car when they pulled you over again.

Facing hard time, you knew it was time to go.
If only Judas were there to kiss you goodbye.

Contrition

Heart burst like water.
Ribs caved in like jars of clay.
Teeth exploded in shards.
Brains become jelly.
Bones become dust.

Accipe signaculum doni Spiritus Sancti[13]

A note left behind on the seat of a car on a bridge over the river.

Ascension

Now, the quiet trees. Now, the darkness.
Now the odor of iron and wet stone
rising in the cool June air.

In Memoriam Annum

for Anselm Hollo

The crows still
gather in the trees
of Herring Run
in the evenings—

not like they did
as you were dying,
but enough to remember
the view of them,
the branches suddenly
leafed-out in black,
the sound of their racket
in the gloaming.

Not much has happened,
or perhaps a lot,
depending on whether
you laugh or cry
at the news.

So what is the news?
A fox has been hunting
in the snow
in our front yard
in Baltimore.

The sun shines madly
through wind chill.

Everyone moves about

as if you had
never mattered.

Cromwell Valley

Curling slowly along the old road,
lightning bugs punctuating the grass,
I pass alone, windows down, under
silent heat lightning tickling the belly
of a storm passing north, dark anvil cloud
scraping against the last glow of day,
late spring. Next to the road, the swollen
sound of water crashes its soft fury
over Loch Raven Dam. A bat darts
under halogen street lamp.

Darkness filters into the valley. Grassy
breeze from cut hay of a close farm
wends across the nameless lower dam,
mingles with pockets of sassafras,
sweet root scent, and the humid air
now cool on tired skin following
a long, warm day. Frogs chirrup along
Towson Run in the wooded slopes above.

Earth smell, familiar as my wife's skin
and breath in bedroom stillness after
making love, envelops me like womb,
like memory. Forty-three years I have
known these woods, this place, its
comfort. Headlights cut through
thin wisps of fog. Skynyrd reels
from the Iron Horse Tavern as I
cross the one-lane stone bridge
and approach the turn north,
up the valley, towards home.

Coma

Boulder, Colorado, November 1996

That Lisa of last summer
I miss her and her dreams
...talks of great plans
eyes wide and alive.

    –Lisa Hammond, "Tired Words and Phrases"

1.

While she short-circuits on a steel gurney somewhere out of sight,
social workers, doctors and a chaplain surround us. "Performing
'heroic efforts' . . . chances of surviving are poor." Into a small
side room. Empty Kleenex boxes. Dour looks. Silence.

Chaplain decides prayer might help. We hold hands in a circle,
heads bowed. Something about "God comfort her." Kind prayer
trained in caution. The news is bad: pulmonary embolisms,
open heart surgery, still too early to tell. We think only

of Lisa. Parents in Michigan are notified by phone. Unbearable
silences. Despair. Nothing inside. What do but cry? No one knows
but us. The weight of a million planets settles on our shoulders.
Hours pass. Doctors prep. We leave through automatic doors

to break the news to friends. Dark clouds obscure the hilltops.
Snow falls gently in surreal gray light.

2.

Thursday night vigil in the outer waiting room. Incense and
candles burn. We feel you with us, out of body. Friday returns
you to body to make a stand against death. Outside, the snowfall
stops. No change over the weekend. Sky stays slate both days.

Monday, the nurse allows us back. We talk to you, hold warm
hands. Chest tubes removed, color's much better. Unswollen face.
Hair pulled back in a scrunchie. You breathe on your own sixteen
times a minute. Nurse says the E.E.G. looks a little better.

Machine breathes ten times a minute. Heavy sedation allows us
to talk to you. Shoulder moves as if a shrug. Slight leg twitch.
Sometimes, involuntary mouth bites down on air tube. Vital signs
have stabilized. Eyes open slightly. Tear rolls down left cheek.

Tuesday sun is warm and dry, snow almost gone. Sedatives reduced.
Still sleeping eyes open halfway and blink. Tenuous hope.

3.

Five days later, it's cold again. Ice on streets and windshields.
Thursday, the neurologist said, "If she wakes, she'll encounter
significant problems." Without sedation, the seizures have
increased. Violent spasms and jerks. Machine still gives her

breath. Catheter streams yellow. I.V.s drip myriad solutions
into passive veins. Her parents settle into routine occupation
of intensive care waiting room. I pray to a God who sits
back and watches. Deliver us not into tomorrow hooked

up to monitors of death suspended. What matters is only
what happens today. Today I crawl out of bed to make coffee,
raise the blinds to overcast sky, let them fall with a crash.
Bills to pay, mountains of laundry, three days no shower, dishes
pile up in the sink. Back into warm sheets, disinterested.

So difficult to do the easy things. Today can wait.

4.

Fourteenth day: the neurologist says the E.E.G. is worse.
"Massive damage, widespread throughout the brain. *If* she wakes
up, she'll be a vegetable. Not much more than that." Your dad
says second neurologist's opinion comes next Monday or Tuesday,

then a meeting Wednesday to discuss where to go from there.
Today an I.V. of opaque blue fluid disappears into your right
nostril. Ubiquitous metal box whishes quiet breath into your
lungs. Tranquility broken by flinches restrained. White gauze

patch on chest. Tomorrow is Thanksgiving. Meteorologist says big storm looms in Pacific Northwest, heavy snow here this weekend.

It is said that every storm takes something with it.
It is said that every storm leaves something behind.

What violence this job of living is.

Saudade: 1983

February

The weathermen had tracked its march across
the continent for days, watched it scoop moisture
from the gulf and turn up the coast, slamming
into winter so hard it exploded snow. They said
it wasn't a blizzard, but we knew different.
Thundersnow and sleet and lightning swirling
above our soaked and frigid fingers, we shaped
the nor'easter into a room four boys could cram their
hearts into. We were powerful, solid in all that white,
self-reliant in snow pants and extra socks and eyes
tearing in the icy wind. Down in that little gully
by the kitchen of your father's church, we made our
stand against God and nature's anger, working stinging
hands that were well past frozen, our toes long given
away to frost inside our ice-block boots. Panting steam
like thoroughbreds, we crawled inside our polar womb.
Cross-legged in silence against the history raging
around us, we saw the work in each other's faces,
the four of us feeling for the first time the real
potential packed in our arms. We sat a long time
in that hut, knowing the use of work, listening to the
violence of what waited for us outside, emerging
just as the winds died to struggle our separate ways
home through waist-high drifts to warm living rooms
and baths, and steaming mugs of instant chocolate.
That night we plummeted into achy sleep, never more
alive, having met peril bigger than us and made it ours.

June

In June we were all sweat and shovels,
delving ourselves down into the cool ground,
covered up by plywood and old rugs and earth
in the back corner of your yard between forsythia
and white pine, where the neighbor's fence dissolved

in barbs and rust. We sat in the darkness, talked of
girls and bikes and music. We wore brown clods home
to dinner in our hair and under our nails, a bucketful
in each shoe, ochre clay smeared into our shirts.
I think often of our fort with its rooms and alcoves,
shelves carved into side walls, candle chimneys
and food stashes, nestled between roots. Alive
in that subterranean shadow world, we dug our
collective grave together, escaping life above
for a little while, for just long enough.

August

That last August Saturday morning before
we returned to gym uniforms and lunch money
and homework for another school year, Steve's
brother Howard drove us in the squeaky yellow
Chevy Nova with black pleather seats that melted
onto the backs of our bare thighs and dropped us
off upstream, ten miles north into horse country.
Shoulders slung with fat old truck tire tubes, we
descended the weedy banks to the Gunpowder,
low in spots after weeks of drought, and set
ourselves into the clear currents. Summer

leaned over us from the riverbanks, green-dappled
and leafy, silent and still. In the cooler, humid
stream bottom, Converse All-stars reeking
of algae and swelter and soaked through, our
heels trailed vees behind us as we drifted
backwards towards autumn, aimless as leaves.

Rambling awkward as foals over pebbled shallows
and ages, chuting fast down the old wooden mill
race between boulders, we were still boy enough
for splash battles and laughter, skipping flat
stones, and mooning everything that moved.

Each of us was Huckleberry Finn. Each of us
was runaway Jim. High school and college and real
work loomed like cops and grandfathers, but we

held the years before us at arms' length, shut our
eyes, floated across those waning hours like
milkweed silk. Covered in dreams and lies, we
leaned our ears into the distance for a sound
that would call us away to ourselves from
futures that would choose us, from the
demons we would not outgrow.

The Investment Building

Rises on an unincorporated suburban
hilltop where, after I was born, strangers'
hands received me in a state agency buried
in its concrete basement. Five months later,
my parents pulled me out of that cold
anonymous drift in dark quiescence
from a bare room behind a two-way mirror.

First baby they saw. Love. Start the paperwork.

They named me for the Hebrew, *gift of God*,
and learned that, to swaddle something more
than a cast-off bag of bones, fat, and skin,
the nurses had given me the same name.

And what of this gift, this alignment of stars
and planets? What if I had been second in line
at that moment, seen and claimed by lesser people
the night before, chosen to not-be by a mother
I have never met who instead carried her
mistake, my origins, inside her, more growth
than fruit, more payload than gift?

Relay sensors shaped like giant powwow
drums were hung on the rooftop signal tower
of the building, facing the four directions.
Growing up, I imagined them beating a signal
to the world that I was there, alive. I pictured
a tribe of orphans far away stomping a dusty circle
to the drums every time a new baby went home.

Forty-four years: the drums on the tower are gone.
Where I once slept numbered and alone, a valet garage
serves a farm-to-table where swinging doors to the restrooms
have two-way mirrors. Coming out, you see only yourself,
but those on the other side can see you, and make plans
accordingly for how to negotiate your emergence
into the light, into the larger space beyond.

Curfew

After the Baltimore riots, April 27, 2015

From the Old French, *covrefeu*, literally, [it] covers
[the] fire. See *cover*. See *fire*. Hear the church bell
toll the hour to cover the hearth fire with ashes
to prevent conflagrations from untended fires.
His eyelids swollen shut; the police van a sealed casket.
The lids of ten thousand prescriptions, empty pill-bottle
shells looted from pharmacies under flickering streetlight.
See what burned under the cover of night, what simmered
under the cover-up. See smoke signals rise at the edge of sky.
Spell it with a blanket that covers and uncovers. Spell
conflagration. Write *the destructive burning of a building,*
town, or forest in blood-soot across the underbellies of ten
thousand vacant clouds. Spell *mayday*, that muscle-sear
of rage. Spell *justice*, that bitter ache. Hear sirens long
into the dark hours, then the odd quiet of empty streets.
Taste the legacy of corpses in the embers glowing at dawn.

Saratoga Passage, August 2014

Whidbey Island, Puget Sound

Up late, I watch the Perseids etch their brief furies through
high, cold, moonlit air. My wife of eleven years, partner of
twenty-one, sleeps in the room behind me. Three stories down,
the salt tide slides away from concrete bulwarks, slips quietly back
into itself: the air's fragrance leavens with life and decay as twelve
hours of water give way to rocks maned with kelp, sand rivulets
emptying under carcasses of hundred-year-old driftwood,
the distinct whiff of an uneaten fish, speared by talons, dropped,
bottom-sunk until now. In two days I will be forty-three. I know
nothing of my birth, hold no narrative of my making, nothing
of the weather that day, what you wore, who drove you
to the hospital. Above, particles ricochet in skips and scratches
through the dark emptiness between stars. I must have been
like these: a brief interrupter of cycles, growing for nine moons,
released out of you and away into space, gone but for an umbilical
scar, fading into the sea of darkness and memory, covered
by the rhythm of tides, washed by time into something smooth
you carry, but cannot touch. A loon at the bend trills across glassy
currents; sound of wingtips in flight touching calm water.
The soft heartbeat of waves lapping the receding tideline grows
fainter as the frozen cosmos delivers hot specks into fleet fire.
I listen as ocean and moon sway their eternal slow dance,
one drawing the other closer, then releasing. I have known
this pulling-to and letting go, the profound momentary ripples,
the lonely stillness that follows. I have known the searing
white heat of entry into this world alone.

The Last Hours of Summer

North Central Railroad Trail, Gunpowder River, Maryland

Already the air has chilled. In the last hours of summer,
September light lingers crisp on wood barnsides bleaching
under the dry blue dome. What bends to hold us, what filters
through us, what remains of us as the winds shift? What of us
recedes in the pewter horizon haze? A lone crow punctuates
the meadow below the old railway bridge. Snapping turtle
big as a hubcap lolls downstream with the current over
gravel bed shallows. Acorns knock through oak branches
down to the soft loam. Slow crickets trill in the cold shade.

In a field by the far road the first rows of fat, ripe corn fall
between giant mechanized pincers, then stillness in the corduroy
of stubble left behind. The empty ache. Brisk sigh lifts the canopy
along the river's edge. The crow, languid fragment of smoke,
lifts from the meadow, dissolves like thought into the afternoon.

Halfpipe, July 1989

Harford County, Maryland

After those evening skateboard sessions, Steve sat in the grass
next to the halfpipe on Derek's farm, kneepads around his ankles,
cuddling Cinder in his lap, its flash-white wiggle-plug Jack Russell
terrier body straining to lick his face. Steve's eyes were lucid when
we skated together, unfucked-up from 'shrooms, acid, and pot.

Dressage horses stood at the pasture fence, their muzzles drooped
over the top rail to watch us skate the ramp. Cinder would chase
us, curved wall to curved wall, ducking our urethane wheels as we
fought gravity that summer after graduation. Steve was always tender
with the dog, and gentle, the dog wanting more of him the more
he gave himself to it. The evenings murmured soft and quiet.

Drenched in sweat, streams of it pouring from our helmets as we
squeezed them against our foreheads, we'd watch the sun set
from the deck of that ramp, the wide scarlet orb vaporizing into
blue pewter haze, humid scent of alfalfa and horseshit sweetening
the air as a cricket symphony rose to meet the lowering night.

All of it comes back to me: the stone taste of minerals in the water
from the well pump next to the ramp, cold and pure as a glacier,
the rhythm of our bodies raging back and forth across plywood,
punctuated by silence as we broke from earth, that boring
flatness, our muscled and tendoned frames straining for flight.

In September, Steve would leave for college far away.
He would get clean, marry, ace law school, move to Colorado,
lose touch. That summer floated, lost in the ether drift of memory
nearly thirty years until a friend's e-mail: found in a heap
at the bottom of Eldorado Canyon, two hundred feet down,
no ropes, no harness, Steve had finally surrendered himself
to that ancient force we had so desperately tried to escape
beside the undulating meadow those sticky evenings,
cradled between two parentheses, ground releasing us
into the sky for a few fleet heartbeats, our world
not yet having crashed into life's unavoidable pull.

Winter Storm Warning

for Steve

The leading fingers of the next coastal storm
reach over the trees at the edge of the ravine,
thin tatters like battle flags; smoke from fire
a long way off. This will be like that storm
in 1983 when I spent the night in your old
stone house on the church grounds. The
weathermen kept revising snow totals
upward until forecast became irrelevant
and we acquiesced to the raging blizzard
that formed over our heads, and what
we could not see piled up around our legs
like paralysis, acceptance. How quietly
the clouds overtook you, hurt accumulating
in drifts over time. What does surrender feel
like as the sound of dry wind fills your ears
as two hundred feet become one hundred
become ground, become silence? The cable
channel has named this storm after the God
of War. How fitting, the white flag of snow
that will cover the world with irony, as the
cannons in my heart continue to pound away.

The Color of the Fluid in My Father's Catheter Reminds Me of Snowball Flavors

1.

When I arrive, my father is standing behind
a sliding curtain, a frail question mark bent
with pain, trying to fill a plastic jug, a trickle
the color of root beer issuing forth from his
body. His appendix has burst, the infection
invading his abdomen like a bio-terror event,
spiking his fever despite the antibiotics. He
is barely coherent, his gentle voice softened
further by circumstance. He seems thinner
in the cheap cotton hospital gown, a skeleton
draped in a shroud. It will be hours before
the doctors operate; weeks until I know
whether they saved his life. I will memorize
the path from the doors to the surgical recovery
unit, when at night the entrance gate stops
charging to park in their garage, the names
of all the nurses in his ward, the words I would
whisper in his ear before he slips away.

2.

In the circular photo from the endoscope,
a cauterized ridge runs where my father's
appendix used to reside, pink and healthy,
a welded seam in body space. Next to it,
the before circle: the appendix, blooming
white on one end like a popped zit, like
a stepped-on éclair. In the CT scan,
a mass in his bladder they choose to ignore
while saving his life. I follow the path
of destruction backwards through his gut
and time: the obstructed bowel from the

distended bladder, bloated from the swollen
prostate, one lobe enlarged the size of a tennis
ball, barnacled with tumors that pathology
calls cancerous a week later. The porthole
scope images show tissue scorched black:
a well-done steak, a field where a wildfire
flared. I imagine the sound of the sizzle,
the sweet scent of my father's burning flesh
as it reaches the surgeon's nostrils; I imagine
my father's remains smoldering on a pyre,
ashes where once his hands oiled baseball
gloves, drew pictures of Mahatma Gandhi
on my lunch bag before school in sixth grade,
held me to his shoulder those first months
after my adoption, patting me gently as I
vomited formula down his back. The screen
over his shoulder shows his heart rate, each
peak on the green line a reassurance, each rise
along the mountain range a gift. I check his
catheter. The mass in his bladder still bleeds;
thick, black cherry flows through his urine tube.

3.

One evening between surgeries, we
analyze the Ravens' draft picks, recall
Manny Machado's homer in the Orioles' win
against Chicago. Portobello clots float and flap
like miniature manta rays in his ostomy bag,
the fluid in the tube draining from his penis
the color of a raspberry snowball. I remind
him of the stone they found in his kidney.
"That's Sisyphus' boulder," he says. "God
thought it would be more convenient to shrink
it so I could carry it around for a while."

4.

Awash in clammy fluorescent light
after his second surgery in ten days, I
watch him sleep, praying for clear fluid
in the catheter tube, remembering the years
after mom left, his slumped form in the dim
cave of our basement watching old *M*A*S*H*
reruns and fighting sleep, head snapping
back, exhausted, the flickering white noise
of the television harmonizing with his snores
as he sank into his deep, green sleep chair
after another day of ad work at the agency,
returning home to angry, scarred, and drifting
children, a toxic brownfield of a marriage bed.

Slowly over hours, his tube lightens to egg custard,
his favorite flavor, then clear. I stand to leave,
step into the quiet, antiseptic hallway where dark
pulmonary monitors loiter in the corners, and turn
back to watch his chest rise with breath and fall,
rise and fall, wondering when the metaphors
will finally drain from his body.

What to Do When Someone Shoots Up a
Gay Nightclub in Florida in the Name of God
While You Are Living at an Artist Colony

The sun is so bright it leaves no shadows
only scars carved into stone on the face of earth

    –U2, "One Tree Hill"

No solace in the red wing blackbird's
requiem to the sky from the fence post,
nothing in the Blue Ridge mountains
shrugging in distant June haze. No
comfort in the grip of nervous skinks
on the cinder block arches darting away
as I pass. The morning walk from bedroom
to studio is a funeral procession, and I bear
the weight of my body like a casket.
Magnolias' sweet breath, boxwoods'
stately musk cannot perfume the rot
of the news. The sun is a muzzle flash
on my cheek, its brightness an insult.

You can choose to feel horror every day,
I remind myself, and think of home, three
hundred toe tags a year on brown men's feet,
so much cold freezer meat for Charon to pole
across to dark shores. Tall meadow grasses
undulate in the hot air. Rabbits scatter into
the weeds as I approach, gravel crunching
like bones underfoot. Above, under God's
blue unblinking eye, vultures pirouette
patiently on thermals, confident the day
will bring a nourishing meal before long.

Reverse Bachata

The blood sucks back from the dance floor into his
mouth, into his nose, his body uncrumples and he stands,
the round stops bouncing around inside his cranium,
stops turning his brain to jelly, gray matter pulls and folds
back neatly into his skull through his cheek, bullet closing
his skin behind it as it leaves him, backs through a woman's
shoulder blade and out of her chest, so fast now, spinning back
into the barrel of the man's AR-15, explosion of gunpowder
re-condensing as the firing mechanism eases away from the
round, trigger moves forward, finger relaxes, and he walks
backward out of the club into the darkness, opens his trunk,
slides it back into the case, un-parks his car and returns
home, walks backward from his car to his apartment door,
slips quietly back into bed, time reverses faster, the sun
unsets for a do-over, he grabs his Quran instead of his gun,
reads Mohammad's verses on tolerance and grace, his pain
lifting like an azan, calls his father to tell him something he won't
want to hear, but must, because the sound of a father weeping
for a son who has accepted himself is preferable to the sound
of forty-nine others' loved ones weeping because their sons
and daughters are now dead, and won't be coming home
late after dancing the night away at the club ever again.

Afternoon at a Gas Station

Luke 10:25-37

Gaunt tweaker with earthquake hands
junkie-trots to cars pulling up to the pumps
hard by the interstate, sinkhole cheeks sucked
in, tired face and forearms pockmarked like
embassy walls in Kabul: the old war blooming
vermilion in poppy fields and syringes, waged
daily in veins collapsed into trenches and a mind
gone thin as bone under tanks rattling the dry Kunduz.
She staggers from the bullet-proof pay window with a pack
of smokes and lies, unwraps each hope, lights it on fire,
inhales every circumstance that led to this corner
a block from the city dump, commerce coursing past
on I-95 at eighty miles an hour, blurred river of rubber
and aluminum exhaling carbon monoxide, carrying
the lucky from purpose to purpose. Polished mahogany
skin glinting like leather in the sun, back broken
and bent, she begs me for change while her pimp
lurks in the shadowed doorway of the car wash.
"Sorry," I say to the tops of my shoes, shaking
the last few drops from the nozzle as if at a urinal.
The skull with caves for eyes turns and shuffles off,
a refugee from a place where she never belonged,
her numbed compass set for another shore, landfall
drawing further away with each unsteady tack.

Years

after Kenneth Rexroth

I come back to the colonial stone house on
the grounds of Babcock Presbyterian Church
where I spent my childhood with Steve. We
were boys, and did boy things in summer, like
snipe twigs stuck in the slats of picnic tables
with air rifles under elms as old as clouds.

We monkeyed the slender cedar in the corner
of his yard and swayed in the wind at the top,
dug underground forts, scrounged up games
of baseball and football with Phil and Brian.

Summer nights: flashlight tag, amber beams
cavorting among the fireflies. We lit sparklers,
waged water balloon wars, stalked squirrels.

Once, I arrived to meet Steve, screen door
slamming behind his clearing storm after a nasty
row, his wrecked mother's slumped form weeping
a psalm through an open kitchen window.

It's been years since he jumped to his death
half a continent away, years more since I
set foot in this yard. I stand at the metal
gate, mid-afternoon, early September.

The old elms raise their tired arms to the hot sky.
We were strong then. We were makers of worlds.

Dark Matter

after Anne Waldman

It is late at night, Blue Ridge hill country, early June.
Mountain breeze carries meandering ribbons of hay,
magnolia, and boxwood throughout the artist colony.
Windows in the barn studio complex cast fluorescent
wedges into the soft lawn as artists move about inside,
speaking in voices of gesture and thought. I am outside
on the gravel path near the barbed fence line, getting away
from my own mind, gazing up, past the tree stand glittering
with constellations of fireflies seeking mates in a delicate
ballet of mute stars edging the abandoned pasture.

Satellites track the earth's outer rim far overhead, steady
grain-specks of carbon and metal bouncing our voices
back to us in calculus, the codices of numbers, lifeblood
of infinity. Beyond, an endless ocean of remote suns
filling the night to the four horizons blinks through ozone,
their fires long extinct before our planet cooled.

Out in the cold, galactic hyper-silences float the echoes of being;
in the nowhere fathoms of absolute zero, the absence of luminosity
is proof of light itself, gone radiance from suns we will never see,
their calidity hurtling away faster than visibility, pulling darkness
inside-out, bending time around itself like confused water.

Hope, too, like light, jukes our reach, an elusive denizen of quasars
and gamma pulses teasing us with curtains of color at the outposts
of consciousness, calling us forth into the black, blind and helpless
as comets, trailing icy pieces of ourselves as we circle the bright
and heavy things that shape, refine, and reduce us. Still, I have
no choice but to seek the glow, drag it back, wrap its warm
plasma tightly around my skin to fend off the void.

Fox barks in the woods, her lone plea reaching me like a keen.
Headlights approach on the farm road and turn, two eyes
receding into the enveloping hush.

Virginia Center for the Creative Arts
2016

Summer Grass Aches and Whispers[14]

Hay-scented fern was the first to go,
turning golden late August, melting
back into shadowed streambed. Now,
poplars begin to drop their leaves: hand-
sized sun catchers, green sails waving
in the solar wind since spring, float down
like sheaves of parchment, brown crunch
shuffling underfoot in the mown grass.
The path ducks into the woods. Acorns tick-
tock through oak boughs, knock to the ground
with a thud. Chainsaw growls at the sunset
along the next ridge over where houses crouch.
Brown loam, loose rocks, cricket song in roots.
There is bone in the cool air by the stream.
Spears of light jab through columns of trunks
where 1950s junk hulks rust in slow oxygen
burn amidst the weeds jutting up through engine
blocks and seat coils. Off in the treetops, barred owl
hoots and takes flight as I emerge at woods edge.
Summer grass aches and whispers its last devotions
to the darkening pasture, a cloud of grateful
breath escaping through my parted teeth.

Ways of Looking at 13 Dead Bald Eagles

1.

Powerline harpy. Pol Pot of the fish. Chittering hookbeak.
Razortongue. Clawfeet. Carrion-gleaner. Money symbol
clutching fascia of arrows and wheat. White-hooded
brownshirt perched in poplars.

2.

A dying species after DDT, eggs made delicate, fragile, easily
shattered, like peace. Thin, like democracy. Like a veiled threat.

3.

Dichloro-diphenyl-trichloroethane:

• *Known to be very persistent in the environment.*
• *Will accumulate in fatty tissues.*
• *Can travel long distances in the upper atmosphere.*
• *Rats become sterile after being fed DDT.*
• *Mice fed low levels of DDT have embryos that fail to attach
to the uterus and irregular reproductive cycles. The offspring
of mice fed DDT have a higher mortality rate.*
• *One of the breakdown products of DDT, DDE3, causes
thinning of eggshells in birds.*[15]

4.

Ripples of bay water where once a fish seined plankton through gills.
Feathers scattered in the halls of Congress: lobbyists' blank checks.

5.

Your call returning like slow glaciers, like dreams,
like stories of the old ways. Ova hardening under safeguard
of the law. Like diplomatic immunity in the clouds.
Like witness protection.

6.

Thirteen colonies fighting for a big idea.
Thirteen men in Jerusalem following a new God.
Said the eagle to her flock: *take this, all of you, and eat it.*

This is my body, which I have given up for you.

7.

He is a Bird
of bad moral Character.
He does not get
his Living honestly.
Too lazy to fish for himself,
he watches the Labour
of the Fishing Hawk;
and when that diligent Bird has
at length taken a Fish …
the Bald Eagle pursues him
… and takes it from him.
With all this Injustice,
he is never in good Case
but like those among Men
who live by Sharping & Robbing
he is generally poor
and often very lousy.

Besides he is a rank Coward:
The little King Bird not bigger
than a Sparrow attacks him boldly
and drives him out of the District.
He is therefore by no means a
proper Emblem for the brave

and honest....[16]

8.

Times Beach. Cuyahoga. Love Canal.
Three Mile Island. Deep Water Horizon. Chesapeake Bay.
Man and raptor alike dine on fish clutched from the same waters.
Pluck out the septic eyes first to blind the prey and nourish the self.
Savor her delicate roe, future mutant offspring sacrificed
to the mouth and beak. Save her heart for last: swallow it whole,
still beating its last precious drops of mercuric blood as it slides
down your hungry gullet.

9.

Perched atop a family totem built
to stand, rot, and return to the earth.
How do we thrive amidst the fetid decline?

10.

Skulls of salmon miles inland, upslope on mountainsides under
Douglas fir. Fertilizer of forests. Cycle keeper. Bringer of life.

11.

*Haliaeetus leucocephalus: Numbers declined seriously
during the first two-thirds of the 20th century.*

*Shooting was one major cause; even after the eagles
were given full legal protection, they continued to decline,
from the effects of DDT and other persistent pesticides.*

*Following the banning of DDT, numbers
have been increasing gradually since the 1970s.*

*Opportunistic; sometimes a predator, sometimes a scavenger:
hunting by watching from a high perch, then swooping down.*

*Hunts by cruising very low over sea or land, taking prey
by surprise. Sometimes steals fish from Ospreys
or other birds. Lands on ground to feed on carrion.*[17]

12.

Someone watched as thirteen tore the poisoned
carcass, took flight one last time.

What does a bald eagle feel as its organs liquefy mid-flight?
What is the sound of a national symbol thudding to earth?

How to lift oneself beyond the forces that pull and drag down.
How to fly into the approaching storm.

13.

The rate of acceleration of a bird of prey falling to earth
 is the same as that of a leaf, a woman jumping from a burning
office tower about to collapse, a rock or a rocket entering
the atmosphere of a blue-green planet at night,
its molecules glowing like love, cauterizing the names
of the universe into the monument of darkness closing
around its dwindling spark.

How to Unpack a Bomb Vest

Start with the vest itself, each pocket stuffed with scriptures
and explosives, hatred and nails, belief and batteries. No. Start
with prayer on Friday, or Saturday, or Sunday. No. Search
online for where the materials and the rhetoric were bought.
No. It's at the hardware store, the mosque, the chatroom.
Begin with an olive tree, a way of life, a desert sky. First,
learn a language spoken for thousands of years. Learn its
words for forgiveness, for war, for love. Learn every word
for revenge spoken by anyone who has seen a drone. It is
scrawled in the concrete dust of Aleppo, in pockmarks across
the walls of Baghdad. The source bubbles up from the ground,
black, thick, pungent. Start with the forests of dinosaurs. No.
Start with the treasuries of the west. Look in your gas tanks
for the instructions on demilitarizing sleeveless tops. Drink
the poetry of nomads and scholars for a taste of old bloodlines
and darkness. Walk the back alleys of grievance in the shadows
of pyramids. Cover yourself with hijab and begin with apology.
It is there, in worn carpets and stained coffee cups, in bombed
out hospital wards and torture cells. Dig a hole six millennia
down through generations of soldiers' bones and sacrifices
to God, deep in the cool earth between two ancient rivers,
and get in it. This is where you will find the directions
for grace written in carbon, written in breath, written
in songs whose lyrics the dead have long since forgotten.

End Notes

1. From Lu Chi's *Wen Fu*.
2. Ibid.
3. Partially composed using lines and phrases from "Still Here & Here Again Then Here & Still" by Anselm Hollo.
4. Photo caption from *Time* magazine, December 30, 1991.
5. Wind.
6. Patient dignity.
7. Kenneth Rexroth, "Inversely, As the Square of Their Distances Apart," from *The Phoenix and the Tortoise*.
8. Rumi, "Sky Circles," tr. by Coleman Barks.
9. Su Tung-p'o, from *Selected Poems of Su Tung-p'o*, tr. by Burton Watson.
10. Ibid.
11. Kenneth Rexroth, "She is Away," from *In Defense of the Earth*.
12. Sign taped to the front door at a New Year's Eve party at a house in Charles Village, Baltimore, 2003.
13. Be sealed with the gift of the Holy Spirit.
14. Title is the first line of "Summer Grass" by Carl Sandburg.
15. The U.S. Environmental Protection Agency [https://www.epa.gov/ingredients-used-pesticide-products/ddt-brief-history-and-status].
16. Benjamin Franklin.
17. The Audubon Society [http://www.audubon.org/field-guide/bird/bald-eagle].

About the Author

Matt Hohner holds an M.F.A. in Writing and Poetics from Naropa University in Boulder, Colorado. His work has been shortlisted for the Ballymaloe International Poetry Prize, taken both third and first prizes in the Maryland Writers Association Poetry Prize and won the *Oberon* Prize for Poetry. His work has appeared in *The Moth, Crab Orchard Review, Free State Review, Comstock Review, The Sow's Ear Poetry Review, Mom Egg Review, Cobalt, The Baltimore Review,* and numerous other publications. Hohner has collaborated with local visual artists for *the light ekphrastic*, and Dutch musician/composer Brechtje for an original composition using his poem "How to Unpack a Bomb Vest," performed by the band VONK in The Netherlands in March 2018. Hohner has held a residency at the Virginia Center for the Creative Arts, which was made possible by a grant from the Mid Atlantic Arts Foundation. Hohner lives in Baltimore, Maryland.

Apprentice House Press

Loyola University Maryland

Apprentice House is the country's only campus-based, student-staffed book publishing company. Directed by professors and industry professionals, it is a nonprofit activity of the Communication Department at Loyola University Maryland.

Using state-of-the-art technology and an experiential learning model of education, Apprentice House publishes books in untraditional ways. This dual responsibility as publishers and educators creates an unprecedented collaborative environment among faculty and students, while teaching tomorrow's editors, designers, and marketers.

Outside of class, progress on book projects is carried forth by the AH Book Publishing Club, a co-curricular campus organization supported by Loyola University Maryland's Office of Student Activities.

Eclectic and provocative, Apprentice House titles intend to entertain as well as spark dialogue on a variety of topics. Financial contributions to sustain the press's work are welcomed. Contributions are tax deductible to the fullest extent allowed by the IRS.

To learn more about Apprentice House books or to obtain submission guidelines, please visit www.apprenticehouse.com.

Apprentice House
Communication Department
Loyola University Maryland
4501 N. Charles Street
Baltimore, MD 21210
Ph: 410-617-5265 • Fax: 410-617-2198
info@apprenticehouse.com • www.apprenticehouse.com

www.ingramcontent.com/pod-product-compliance
Lightning Source LLC
Chambersburg PA
CBHW061837040426
42447CB00012B/3013